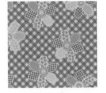

CONTENTS

INTRODUCTION

Quilting is the process of using a simple running stitch to sew together the three layers of any quilted article, from a brooch to a bed quilt. These three layers – called the quilt "sandwich" – consist of a top fabric (which might be patchwork); a middle layer of batting; and a lining fabric.

Quilting is both a functional and decorative means of holding the quilt filling in place. It is a craft ideally suited to the beginner, who can opt either to create a few simple stitches or lines, or to try a more complicated design, such as an ornate shell – or perhaps something in between, a leaf shape, for example. Done by hand or by machine, the quilting of the three layers will give it an eye-catching, three-dimensional quality.

This book also features appliqué, which is the sewing of a cut-out fabric motif onto a background material, which can then be quilted. And, like other titles in the Craft Workbooks series, this one has been prepared with the beginner in mind, taking them through various methods and techniques in straightforward, illustrated stages.

Fabric quilting is thought to go back at least as far as the Ancient Egyptians. In the West, recently found examples from the Middle Ages include padded undergarments worn by knights to make their armor more comfortable and throughout several centuries quilted petticoats, sleeves, doublets and vests provided much-needed insulation during harsh weather. By the eighteenth and nineteenth centuries, however, it was bed covers that received the greatest attention from quilters, warm bedding being essential in the days before central heating.

While uniformly quilted "whole cloth" bed covers were popular in the United Kingdom, a different tradition evolved in the United States. There, quilt tops were sewn from smaller individual pieces into blocks in a huge variety of patterns. Individual blocks were more convenient to sew than large pieces, especially when the sewer was travelling by wagon train. An important part of a bride's dowry was the quilts she had accumulated, especially in the days before manufactured blankets and in areas where wool for blankets wasn't prevalent. Young women often made quilt tops that were stashed away in a chest until an engagement was announced and then family and friends got together at "quilting bees," so the quilts would be complete by the time of the wedding.

Although many people still associate quilting with bed covers, there are other items that can be beautifully enhanced, such as cases for needles, glasses or cell phones, and soft furnishings like cushions or table runners. Plain or patterned fabrics lend themselves to quilting so it isn't necessary to have patchwork as your top fabric.

This book describes many ways to quilt a piece of work, depending on the time you can devote to it and the effect you wish to achieve. There are even some types of quilting – such as sashiko from Japan and kantha from India – that involve stitching together just two layers, omitting the filling layer. Machine quilting, using a quilting foot, is quicker but hand-quilting, with or without a frame, can undoubtedly be more relaxing.

Beginner quilters need not worry unduly about the number of hand stitches per inch but aim initially for the stitches to be spaced evenly and be of equal length. Fortunately there are neither patchwork nor quilting police! It is preferable that the three layers are quilted – whether tufted at intervals, or closely stitched in a pattern – so that your work will be completed rather than remain as a UFO (Unfinished Object). Perfecting your quilting style will come naturally with practise and give you the confidence to try larger pieces.

CRAFT WORKBOOKS

Quilting & Appliqué

A beginner's step-by-step guide to stitching by hand and machine

MARTHA PRESTON

Design Originals

an Imprint of Fox Chapel Publishing

www.d-originals.com

In memory of my very quiltworthy sister, Phee.

Martha Preston was born in the Blue Ridge Mountains, Virginia, USA. Her interest in patchwork and quilting was aroused when she unearthed a red-and-white pinwheel quilt belonging to her grandmother. She completed Part 1 of her City and Guilds in Patchwork and Quilting in 1995 and has been an avid quilt-maker ever since. She specializes in hand-quilting, and especially admires the designs of the Welsh, Durham and Amish communities.

ISBN 978-1-57421-502-1

Illustrated by David Woodroffe
Front cover: Shutterstock
Back cover: Background, Hand quilted patchwork of shirt fabrics.
1 Simple appliqué 2 Quilted and appliquéd tea cosy 3 Trapunto 4 Reverse appliqué
5 Welsh quilting roundel 6 Stained glass appliqué 7 Tied quilting 8 Corded quilting

PART ONE

EQUIPMENT AND MATERIALS

USING A ROTARY CUTTER

How to position the acrylic ruler and rotary cutter when cutting shapes.

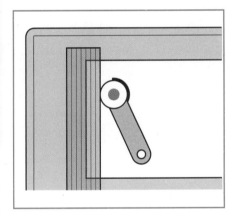

1 Cutting plain strips

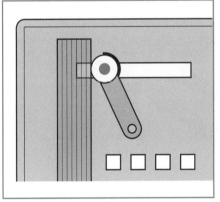

2 Cutting squares

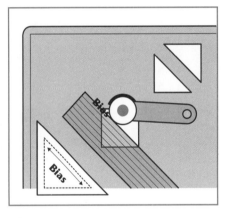

3 Cutting right-angled triangles

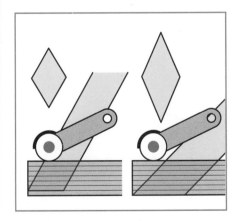

4 Cutting diamonds

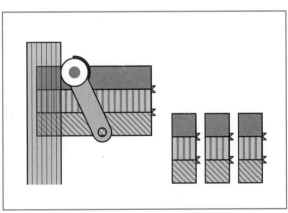

5 Cutting sewn strips

BASIC EQUIPMENT

A "Between" needles for hand quilting (sizes 8–10 are average) and crewel (embroidery) needles for kantha and sashiko

B Pins for basting and appliqué

C Safety pins for basting quilt layers; curved ones can be easier to handle

D Cotton thread for machine sewing; cotton and/or hand-quilting thread (heavier weight) for hand-quilting

E Cotton embroidery thread for sashiko, kantha and tied quilting

F Beeswax, useful when using ordinary cotton or synthetic thread for hand-quilting. Drawing the thread across the wax makes it less prone to tangle

G Thimble

H Small metal or leather stick-on pads help to prevent hand-quilter's callous

I Embroidery scissors for cutting thread and appliqué shapes

J Craft scissors for cutting templates

K Rotary cutter, capable of cutting through batting and up to 6 layers of cotton patchwork fabric. A locking mechanism retracts the blade for safety. Use in conjunction with a cutting mat (L), clear ruler (M) and quilter's acrylic ruler (N), available in different lengths and widths, with a range of markings

O Compass and metal ruler (P) – useful for constructing templates that can be made from recycled plastic or cardboard packaging. Use in conjunction with graph paper (Q)

R Quilter's fabric-marking pen for marking quilt lines or drawing around appliqué shapes on fabric

S Chalk pencil with a brush at the end

T Spray adhesive for basting quilt layers together

U Repositionable adhesive stick for positioning appliqué shapes onto fabric or template material before cutting around them

V Hoop for holding layers to be hand-quilted (see also p. 12)

W Sewing machine

X Iron

FABRIC

Modern fabrics consist of natural or manmade fibers, often mixed to combine their best qualities. Every woven fabric belongs to one of three types.

Woven fabric

1 Plain weave Alternate warp (lengthwise) threads go over one and under one of the weft (crosswise) threads. Linen, poplin, muslin, and organza are familiar examples.

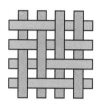

2 Twill weave Interlaces warp and weft threads over and under two or more threads progressively, to produce a clear diagonal pattern on hardwearing fabrics such as denim and gabardine.

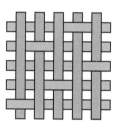

3 Satin weave A smooth, glossy, compact surface created by long silky "floats" that leave no weft visible; the reverse is matt.

Shrinkage

The tighter the weave, the less likely a fabric is to shrink during or after manufacture. The store label will say if a fabric is pre-shrunk. If not, and if necessary, shrink it yourself before use. Wash and dry according to the care label; this will also reveal whether the fabric is colorfast.

The grain

The grain of a fabric is the direction in which the warp and weft threads lie. The warp runs lengthwise, parallel to the selvage; this is the *lengthwise grain*. The weft follows the *crosswise grain*, at right angles to the selvage.

The bias

The bias lies along any diagonal line between the lengthwise and crosswise grains. True bias is at the 45-degree angle, where you will get the maximum stretch. Bias strips are often used for piping and binding edges because of their flexibility on curves and corners.

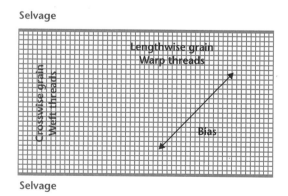

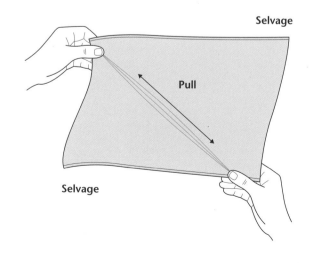

Batting

Batting forms the central layer of a quilted project. It can be made from natural fibers (cotton, wool, alpaca, silk, or bamboo); synthetic (polyester); or a combination of these. It is sold by the yard in various widths and colors. Some filling fibers are more suited to machine-washing while others respond better to hand-washing (always follow the manufacturer's advice). It's clearly preferable to use a machine-washable fiber for a child's quilt.

Weight and thickness 2 oz [60g] is generally the thinnest, followed by 4 oz, 6 oz and 8 oz [115g, 180g and 220g]. One is available weighing less than 2 oz [60g], which enables the hand quilter to work more stitches to the inch.

Shrinkage Synthetic battings shrink very little, if at all. They are good for hand quilting and tying. Natural fibers do suffer shrinkage, which can be minimized before quilting, although some people prefer the crinkled look of their quilt once it has shrunk. Do observe the manufacturer's advice on this.

Which type of batting? Black is available in 100 percent polyester or a cotton/polyester blend for quilts made of dark fabrics. For quilting light fabrics, cotton is available in natural (cream) or unbleached. Wool, silk, alpaca, and bamboo are also usually unbleached. Polyester is available in white. Some natural cotton batting may have seed heads left in it, which may show through the top of a light-colored quilt.

Cost Polyester batting is the least costly, but beware – some cheap products can "beard," which means the act of stitching pulls fibers through to the top. This gets worse if you try to pull the fibers out. In general, cotton and natural fillings "beard" less than synthetic. It is worth buying from a reputable quilt store to obtain a quality batting that "needles" well.

How much to use? For large projects, buy a total of 12 in [30 cm] beyond the length and width of your finished quilt top; for medium-sized projects, a total of 8 in [20 cm] more; and for smaller projects, 4 in [10 cm]. Allow extra batting for the quilt hoop or frame to grip so that you can quilt up to the edge of your project.

Polyester batting can arrive badly creased through packaging. Spread it out flat and use a hair dryer to relax and remove the creases.

Never use synthetic wadding [batting] in an oven mitt or potholder – too much heat can cause it to melt. Cotton towelling is a more suitable alternative.

Fat quarters

A "fat quarter" means getting larger pieces of fabric than are possible from a standard quarter of a yard, including strips twice as long on the lengthwise grain (see figure). The metric system in Europe may not always cater for fat quarters from retailers, but they are readily available online.

This can bring increased variety to your fabric "stash" because they are sold both individually and in sets or "bunches," in coordinated or even contrasting colorways, and also in plains and prints. This means you can buy smaller quantities of fabric that will enhance each other. Whole quilts can be made from fat quarters.

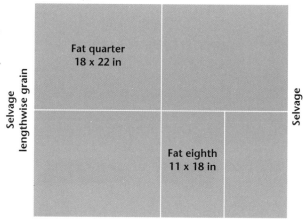

Regular quarter yard, 9 x 44 in

Calculating quantities

The standard widths for fabric are: 36, 44–45 and 54 in [90, 115 and 150 cm]. Dress-weight fabric is usually 44–45 in [115 cm]; muslin and interfacings come in 36 in [90 cm] widths.

Study your pattern. How many different templates does it use? How many patches of each shape? Before calculating, take 2 in [5 cm] off the width for shrinkage and removal of selvages. *Be sure to include seam allowances.*

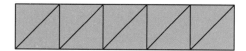

1 See how many times a template fits into the fabric width, then divide that number into the total number of patches required in that particular shape.

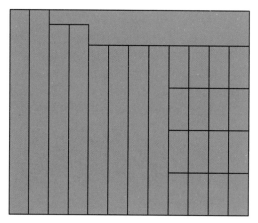

2 Do the same for the number of lengthwise strips for borders and sashing (pp. 34 and 39).

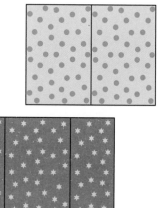

3 Be prepared to piece together two or three widths for lining, according to the quilt size.

To estimate the length of fabric needed after 1 and 2, divide the total number of patches by the number in a single width and multiply the result by the width of the template.

An economical cutting plan takes straight strips from one edge of the fabric and irregular shapes from the other. Bias-binding or piping around the edges uses strips cut on the diagonal, which will lead to some wastage.

THE SEWING MACHINE

A well-built sewing machine will give decades of service if it is properly used and maintained.

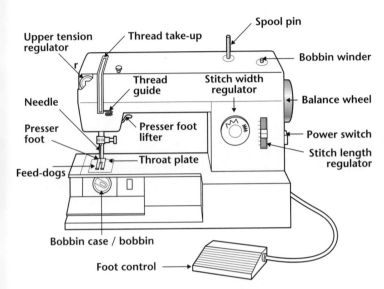

Upper tension regulator · Thread take-up · Spool pin · Bobbin winder · Thread guide · Stitch width regulator · Balance wheel · Needle · Presser foot lifter · Power switch · Presser foot · Throat plate · Stitch length regulator · Feed-dogs · Bobbin case / bobbin · Foot control

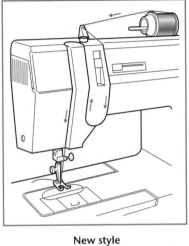

New style

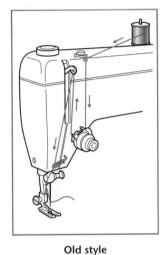

Old style

Regularly clear lint from the feed-dogs and bobbin area. Oil the machine according to the maker's instructions. Avoid bent needles by raising the needle high before removing work and don't drag on it while stitching. Always raise the presser foot while threading the machine and lower it when you put the machine away. *Switch the power off before disconnecting plugs, cleaning, or attempting repairs.*

Newer-style machines incorporate tension disks, thread guides and take-up lever inside their casings, avoiding various steps involved with threading older models. Note that some needles thread from front to back and some from left to right. Incorrect threading is probably responsible for more beginners' problems than anything else. If you have no printed instructions, search for your make and model online, where a huge range of manuals is available.

Four machine feet that can form a basic kit for quilters (see also p. 35):

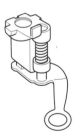

1 Straight-stitch The general-purpose presser foot supplied on every machine.

2 Zigzag Has a horizontal slot to allow for the "swing" of the needle as it forms a zigzag with the thread.

With multiple needles (p.35) use this foot for straight stitching *only*.

3 Darning/embroidery Used in free motion stitching together with lowered feed-dogs and hooped fabric, this sprung foot allows maneuvrability of fabric and close control of stitching while protecting the fingers.

4 Walking/quilting Uses teeth to feed upper and lower layers of fabric together evenly and avoid bunching.

QUILTING FRAMES AND HOOPS

Hoops and frames come in a wide range of sizes and can be held in the lap or clamped to a table. Some are floor-standing and have fully adjustable tilt for ease of use.

For the hand quilter, a frame or hoop is extremely useful because it ensures all three layers are held taut and wrinkle-free, thus reducing the likelihood of any stitches catching a wrinkle on the underside. The three layers still need to be basted with a needle and thread or safety pins. Adhesive basting spray – available from quilting suppliers – may be used instead, but only *very sparingly and in a well-ventilated area.* The adhesive does not gum up sewing needles and washes out easily afterwards.

Once the quilt layers are clamped in a frame, they should be fairly taut but not so tight that the fabric is distorted.

Quilts left in frames can become cat magnets. Even a small cat can distort the layers if it is left to sleep there. Better to reserve a spare quilt for your pet!

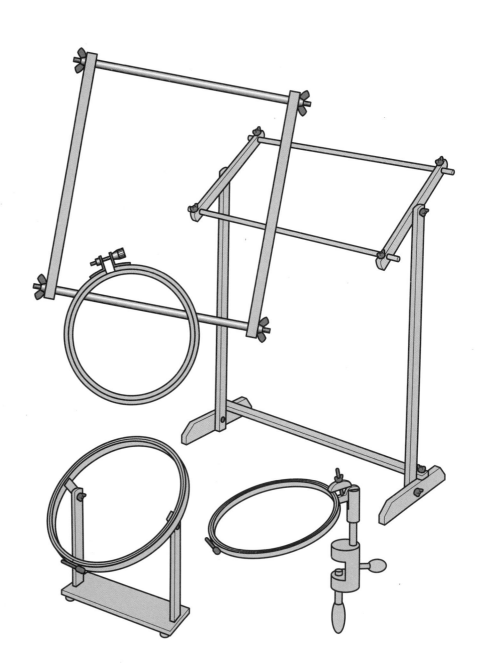

The traditional wooden roller-frame is a floor-standing model that provides a rectangular quilting surface, with two bars or rollers the width of the quilt and two stretchers that keep the layers taut by holding the rollers in place. The disadvantage of this type is that it is extremely heavy and takes up a lot of space.

A handy alternative is the PVC frame, constructed from a plastic tube that resembles plumbing pipe. It provides a large rectangular surface that any size of quilt can be draped over and hand quilted. The quilt layers are held taut by clamping further pieces of piping over the frame's perimeters. A particular advantage is that this type of frame assembles and disassembles easily; the lengths of piping are lightweight and can be stored together in a bag between quilting projects and carried anywhere.

In order to work to the very edge of your quilt, baste additional strips of fabric to the sides of it, and use extra batting so the hoop or frame has something to grip. This ensures that the main quilting area remains within the frame's perimeters and not so near the edge that it becomes impossible to quilt. This technique is also useful if you are quilting a project much smaller than your frame or hoop. Remember to check the underside of your quilt frequently to ensure a wrinkle hasn't appeared.

When not quilting for a period of time, such as overnight, it is important to remove your quilt from the frame or at least substantially loosen it. If left clamped in a frame for too long, the layers will become overstretched and go baggy.

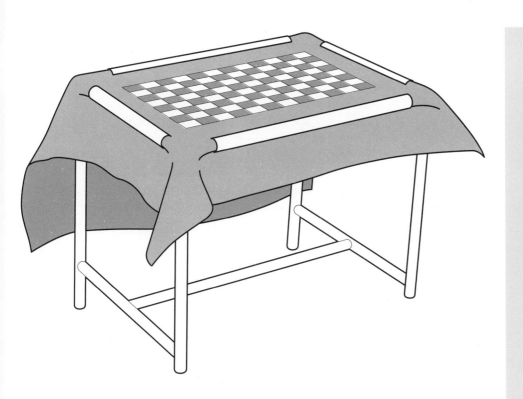

"Lap quilting" without a frame is possible provided all layers are thoroughly basted to prevent them shifting. This useful combination of a cutting mat with a soft ironing surface on the reverse can also double as a lap support.

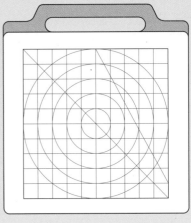

QUILTING OUTLINES

A selection of ideas for stitched outlines, both traditional and contemporary.

PART TWO:
QUILTING METHODS AND TECHNIQUES

QUILTING BY HAND AND MACHINE

This section covers both hand and machine quilting methods and techniques, as well as the different effects possible with quilting.

First it is important to consider whether your project and the time you have available lends itself to hand quilting or machine quilting. Indeed, both methods can be used on the same piece of work. It is also a matter of personal preference; some prefer the "rhythm" of hand quilting and find it calming, while others feel more at home quilting with their sewing machine.

Machine quilting is quicker on larger projects such as bed quilts. It is also preferable for quilts that will need frequent washing, such as those for children or pets. However, unlike hand quilting, it means you are tied to the room where your sewing machine is, and it is tempting to spend so long machine quilting that you may find yourself suffering from shoulder or neck ache; do take frequent breaks to stretch your arms and legs. It can also prove difficult to move a large quilt through a machine in order to stitch in a different direction.

Hand quilting a large project will take longer but lends itself to quilting in different directions as it is easier to shift a quilt over a frame or hoop than through a machine. Hand quilting is more portable as the frame can be moved from room to room, taking advantage of natural daylight, and more readily taken on vacation. A combination of machine and hand quilting is a good idea where practical. For example, you could machine quilt between your quilt blocks and along any sashing or borders, but hand quilt motifs in the spaces in between.

Many seasoned quilters prefer to use cotton thread for both hand and machine work because synthetic threads can, over time, wear through natural fibers, thus weakening quilt stitches and causing seams to separate.

If synthetic threads are used at the "piecing" stage (sewing shapes together to form a block) or when creating appliqué, care must be taken not to use a very hot iron, in case the heat weakens the thread so the stitches fail to hold.

THE QUILT SANDWICH

Inserting batting

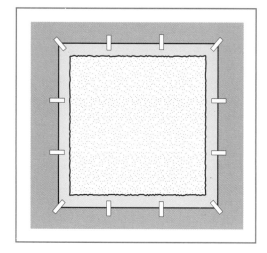

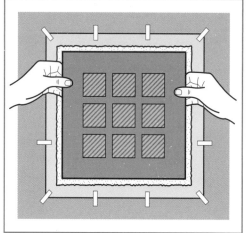

1 Press any seams in a pieced lining (p. 10) WS up, and tape it to a flat surface. Center batting with a margin all round.

2 Having pressed the quilt top quite flat and made sure it is square, place RS up over the batting.

Pinning and basting layers

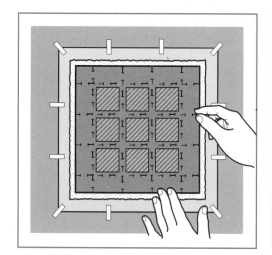

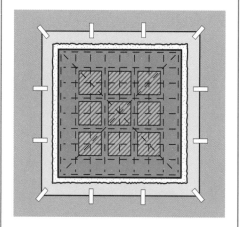

3 Pin all three layers together with long straight pins or large safety pins. You will need plenty for this stage. Alternatively, use a spray-on basting adhesive, following the manufacturer's instructions.

4 Knot the thread end and, starting at the center, baste out towards the edges. First, stitch horizontally and vertically at 4 in [10 cm] intervals; then from the center diagonally to each corner.

> Some materials can be recycled for use as batting, such as a thin blanket or a flannel/brushed cotton sheet. Even a plain cotton sheet can be incorporated in a lightweight summer quilt.

Starting hand quilting

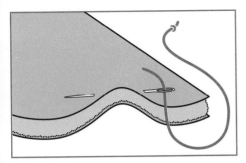 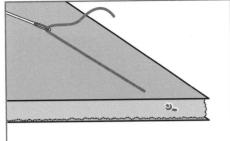 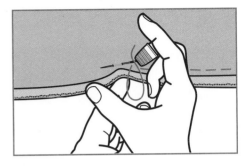

1 Thread a size 8 or 10 "between" needle with thread 12–18 in [30–45 cm] long. Tie a knot in the end. Needle in and out through both top and batting.

2 Pull the thread taut so the knot passes through the fabric to become anchored in the batting. For a firmer hold, tie a double knot.

3 With a thimble, push the needle in at an angle until the finger beneath feels the point through all the layers. The finger below guides the needle back to the surface.

Finishing hand quilting

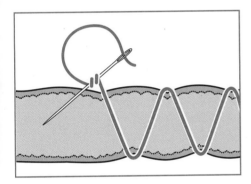 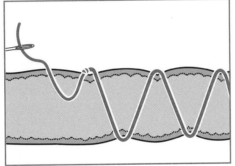 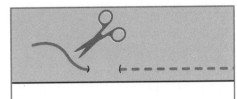

1 Tie a knot close to the quilt's surface, or wind the thread a couple of times round the needle and insert through the top and batting where the final stitch would be.

2 Run the needle through the batting 1 in [2.5 cm] away from the stitching line. Pull the thread taut so that the knot passes through the fabric.

3 Pull the needle and thread gently to the surface and snip the thread close. Pull the fabric until the snipped end disappears below the surface.

Stitching method

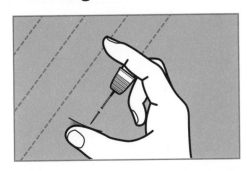 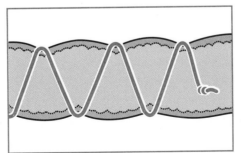 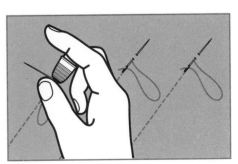

1 Following markings, stitch rows of small, even running stitches through all the layers. Rows no more than 2 in [5 cm] apart ensure the filling stays in place.

2 Stitches will get smaller with practice. Few people achieve the ideal of ten stitches per inch – six is more realistic. Pull the thread taut enough to make indentations in both surfaces.

3 To ensure that you work evenly across a large quilt, try having several needles threaded up at once.

Machine quilting

For quilts too thick to hand stitch: load the machine with No. 40 cotton and a new 90/14 needle; set the stitch length to ten per inch. Choose a top thread that blends with your patchwork and wind two bobbins with a color to match the lining. *Do not use any glazed hand quilting thread,* since the special wax interferes with the tension disks.

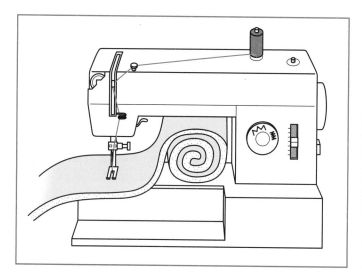

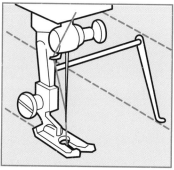

1 Roll the quilt tightly at one end and tuck under the machine throat. You can secure the rolls with clips. Begin parallel lines of stitching at the halfway point along one edge. Start and finish each line with forward and reverse stitches.

2 If you have one, use a walking/ quilting foot (p. 11). A spacer guide usefully sets a regular interval between stitch lines.

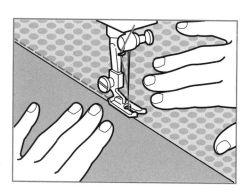

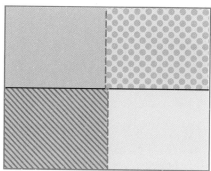

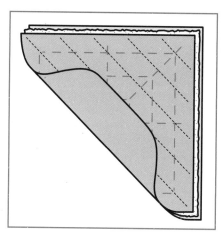

3 Don't drag the quilt as you sew as this causes skipped stitches. Smooth the fabric either side of the needle and go at a steady speed. Check the back for loops or puckers at the end of each line.

4 Ideally, seams should match but you can "jump" a small difference across a join when stitching "in the ditch" (see opposite).

5 Roll the quilt diagonally if sewing diagonal lines. Begin at the halfway point as in Step 1.

In the ditch

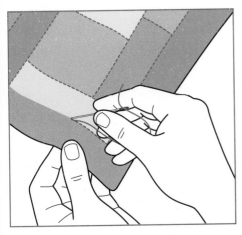 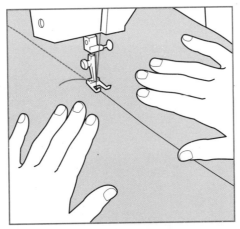

"In the ditch" describes quilting stitches in the center of the seam. It can be done by hand (left) or machine (right) and is useful if you want your project to look quilted but would rather not use elaborately quilted motifs. When you are quilting by machine, the needle can reach the "ditch" area more easily if you use your hands to spread open the seams and employ the walking quilting foot (p. 11). Work with an unobtrusive thread color such as a medium grey or brown, rather than a contrasting shade.

Tied quilting

Tufted quilting is a quick method of holding layers together, although they should still be basted beforehand. Try two colors of knitting yarn knotted together, use bright embroidery floss, or even incorporate buttons *(see rear cover)*.

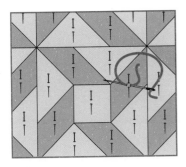 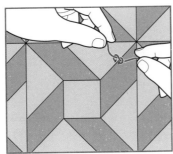 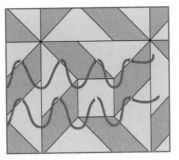 

1 Mark tuft positions with long pins. Single back-stitch around each pin and cut the thread.

2 Tie the free ends in a double knot and trim level.

3 Alternatively, link all the back stitches with generous loops.

4 Cut the loops and knot each pair of ends over the central stitch.

ECHO QUILTING

Echo and contour quilting are similar in that the lines of quilting echo the shape of each appliquéd shape or patchwork piece. For example, if an appliqué features shell or petal shapes, you can add interest by quilting two or more equidistant lines around each one.

Hawaiian appliqué

In this formalized style of appliqué, intricate designs are cut from folded paper and transferred to a plain colored fabric. The fabric is cut out and sewn onto a white background. Quilting afterwards outlines the pattern in multiple rows known as *kapa lau*.

CONTOUR QUILTING

Contour quilting emphasizes the geometric shapes in a patchworked block. Either by hand or machine, sew the decorative stitch lines approximately ¼ in [7 mm] from the seam lines. This technique is also known as "outline stitching."

Echo and contour quilting can be combined in the same project.

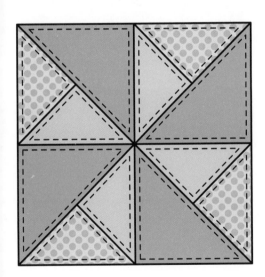

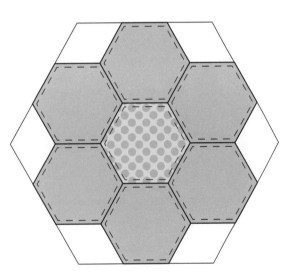

FILLING PATTERNS

Filling patterns are used to quilt large background spaces around individual motifs, or they may be used on their own to quilt an entire project. These overall patterns are an excellent treatment for larger areas, not only for the decorative effect but also to ensure that the batting layer doesn't bunch up.

Straight-line patterns are the quickest. Attach a spacer foot (p. 18) that enables you to stitch parallel lines without having to mark them. Otherwise, use an acrylic ruler and marking pencil to draw quilting lines at regular intervals on your quilt top. The directions on your batting packaging will indicate how far apart the quilting lines can be.

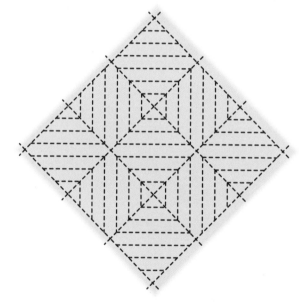

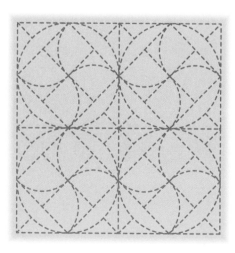

If you want a wavy filler pattern, consider using a circular or oval platter as a template. Place it on your quilt top and draw along one edge, reversing the edge as you go along.

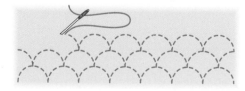

FREE MOTION QUILTING

Free motion quilting (also known as free machine quilting) provides an even quicker filling stitch because it isn't marked out first on the top fabric layer. It functions either as background or as the primary quilting pattern. The traditional wooden hoop (p. 12) can also be used with free motion work; in this case, the rim is turned upward so that the WS of the fabric rests flat against the base plate.

Free motion is performed with a darning or embroidery foot and the machine's feed-dogs lowered or covered with a special plate. Your sewing machine manual will show how to operate the drop feed mechanism, usually via a simple lever. It is an added advantage to use a sprung foot (p. 11) because the vertical spring action prevents the top fabric coming up with the needle each time and lifting away from the batting inside.

Because the tiny metal teeth of the feed-dogs aren't engaged below and you have set your stitch length dial to zero, you are free to move the quilt in any direction through the machine. You will need practise to coordinate the stitch speed and movement of the fabric. It is important to run the machine at a constant speed in order to maintain a consistent stitch length. The general rule is to stitch fast but move the fabric slowly. Use a thread near the color of the top layer if you want the quilting to blend in.

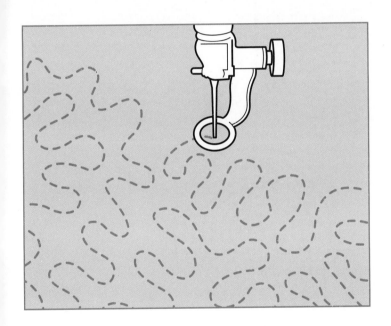

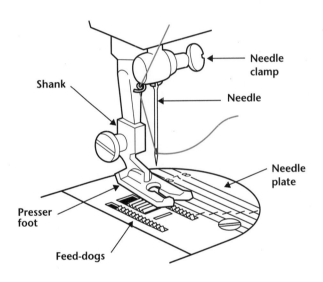

Shank

Needle clamp

Needle

Needle plate

Presser foot

Feed-dogs

KANTHA

Kantha (meaning "rags") is a traditional hand stitching technique from Bangladesh, on the Indian subcontinent, sewn predominantly with a running stitch and usually in different color threads.

It is worked through multiple layers of fine cotton fabric without batting, though you could use a very thin filling material. Thick batting would make the stitches too difficult to pull through.

Kantha uses both stylized motifs and pictorial design. Colored threads are used to stitch the outline of a motif or figure, such as the bird shown here. Then the inside is filled with consecutive stitch lines in various complementary colors. The background is stitched in a thread that matches the color of the background fabric.

As with sashiko (opposite), the kantha stitch method is to pleat the fabric onto the tip of the needle and make as many stitches as possible before pulling the needle through and smoothing out the fabric.

Kantha threads Use a single strand of cotton embroidery thread such as perle [pearl] or two or three strands of floss.

Fabric Choose soft fabrics such as lawn or muslin, which allow ease of stitching. In Bangladesh, recycled sari fabrics are traditionally used in kantha work.

Needle Use a sashiko needle, or a large "sharp" or crewel needle. The eye must be big enough to accommodate thicker strands.

SASHIKO

This Japanese style of running-stitch embroidery is not usually quilted directly through batting but worked through one or two layers of fabric and then backed by a layer of filling and a lining fabric.

Around three centuries ago, Japanese working men and warriors wore indigo-dyed jackets constructed from two layers of hemp or cotton fabric and the women stitched these layers together for durability. They traditionally used white thread on a dark blue background and sashiko needles 2 in [5 cm] long with a uniform shaft. The stitch pattern for everyday wear was fairly plain but they developed elaborate designs for special occasions.

Threads Specialist sashiko threads are generally used double; alternatives are stranded embroidery floss or a shiny pearl twist. The stitches may be longer than for regular quilting – sashiko uses a long running stitch at five or six stitches to an inch – but aim to keep them all the same length.

Fabric Sashiko fabrics have a lower thread count than ordinary cottons, which enables the thread to be pulled through more easily. However, normal cotton patchwork fabrics can be combined with a single thread for the stitching.

Needle As with those for kantha work, a long needle with a large eye is necessary for the thicker threads, for example a large "sharp" or a crewel embroidery needle.

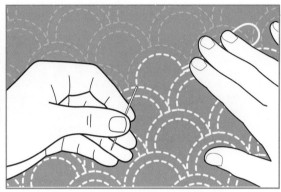

Use your cutting mat, acrylic ruler and marking pencil to draw a grid on a piece of sashiko fabric. Stitch lines can then be devised or you could use a cardboard template to create the curved lines of the shell pattern, for example. Horizontal and vertical lines are usually stitched first and then the diagonals. Any other shapes are done last.

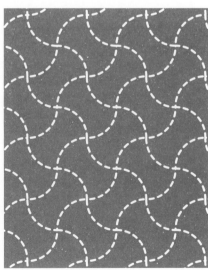

CORDED QUILTING

Sometimes known as Italian quilting, this technique embellishes solid-colored fabrics with a raised design *(see rear cover)*. It has no internal layer of batting.

The corded effect is achieved by sewing twin lines of running stitch through two layers of fabric and then (from the WS) inserting lengths of cord between both the layers and the two lines of stitching.

Apart from a straightforward stripe or lattice design, you might begin with a simple spiral, leaf shape or initial letter. Place a sheet of heavy tracing paper or plastic (Kodatrace) over the original image and trace it. Create a template by cutting out the traced shape.

Position the template on the surface of the fabric and draw a double line round it with a fabric marker pen. Take care to keep the channel between the lines the correct width throughout the design; too narrow, and the cord will not fit; too wide, and the cord will barely show as raised.

Fabrics Use a close-woven plain colored cotton for the top and a looser weave for the backing. The latter makes it easier to enter the stitched channel with the threader. Cut both bits of fabric the same size, including a seam allowance if necessary.

Cord Use pre-shrunk piping cord or candlewick (a thick, soft cotton embroidery thread). Synthetic knitting yarn can also be used.

Needle A bodkin or blunt-tipped needle will serve as a threader, so long as the eye can take the cord and the tip doesn't pierce the fabric in the wrong places. Insert the cord through a loop of ordinary thread and pull both through the eye of the threader.

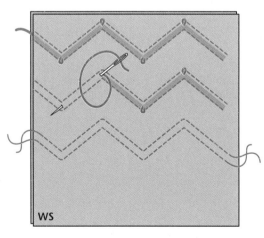
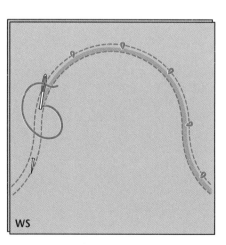
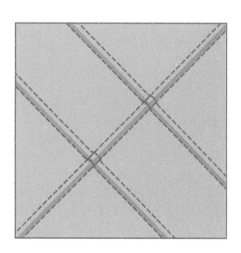

Insert the threader tip into the WS and guide it through the stitched channel, pulling very gently. Where lines cross or bend sharply, the needle and cord are brought out and reinserted, leaving a small loop at the back of the fabric to "ease" and avoid puckering. When complete, leave a short tail of cord (½ in [1 cm]) at the back of the work, not a knot.

Avoid stitching across channels at intersections by using a "jump" stitch on each line (p. 18). If channels are blocked, don't cut the stitching or it will come undone too far. Instead, bring out the cord on the WS on both lines and cross them over before reinserting.

TRAPUNTO

Trapunto is Italian for "embroider." This centuries-old technique is also known as "stuffed quilting," where motifs are padded so that they appear in relief against the background fabric *(see rear cover)*. The raised motifs can be enhanced further by hand or machine stitching a filling pattern over the background area.

Fabric A plain glazed cotton will show up the motifs better than a matt fabric. Alternatively, if you have a themed fabric, featuring shapes such as animals or fruit, you can stitch around these shapes and stuff them through a slit in the backing fabric. Sometimes the backing fabric has such a loose weave that the stuffing can be worked in through it, rather than cutting a slit.

Shadow quilting

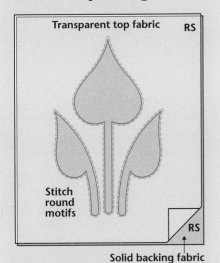

Transparent top fabric   RS

Stitch round motifs

RS

Solid backing fabric

An attractive, delicate effect can be created by sandwiching a different colored material, pre-cut to shape, between a transparent top layer such as voile and a solid backing fabric. It is then contained by hand or machine stitching. Stencil-type motifs are ideal for this technique, which is essentially decorative.

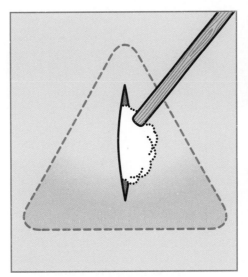

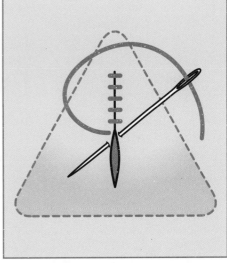

Mark out your motif on the top fabric of a quilt sandwich and then outline it with a single line of stitches through all three layers. The stuffing is inserted through a small slit in the backing fabric. This extra material can be wool, polyester filling, or whatever material is used in the rest of the work. It is best to avoid kapok or cotton balls because they form lumps too easily, especially if the item is to be washed. Use a stuffing stick or small crochet hook to push it into all areas of the motif being stuffed.

Once the areas are packed, close the slit at the back of the work. Hold the two raw edges together and oversew them with broad stitches. Finish by running the thread off into the stuffing. If the back is going to be exposed, as on a quilt, you will need to line the work afterwards.

PROJECT: COASTERS

Simple coasters are an ideal first quilting project and would make a welcome gift.

To make 4 coasters you will need:

- Two pieces of fabric 12 x 6 in [30 x 15 cm] in two different designs for the top surfaces
- One piece of fabric 11 x 11 in [28 x 28 cm] for the backing/lining
- A piece of thin batting 11 x 11 in [28 x 28 cm] for the filling

Make the first coaster Using an acrylic ruler and mat, cut two 3 in [8 cm] squares in two different fabrics to give four squares in total (two of each fabric). Or draw a 3 in [8 cm] square on graph paper and use as a template (this includes a ¼ in [7 mm] seam allowance). Similarly, cut out the backing fabric and batting directly or use graph paper to make a 5½ in [14 cm] square template.

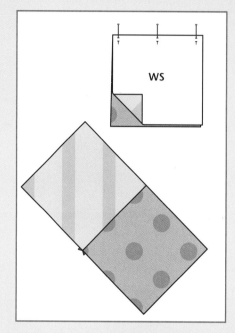

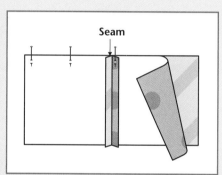

1 RS together, pin and stitch together one square of each fabric with a ¼ in [7 mm] seam allowance to produce two pairs of squares.

2 Ensuring that the different fabric squares fall in a checkerboard formation, place RS together, pin, and stitch the two strips together. Press the seams open.

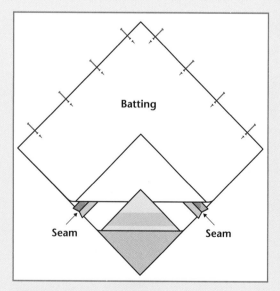

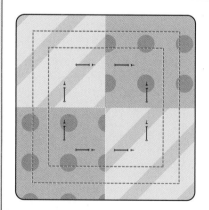

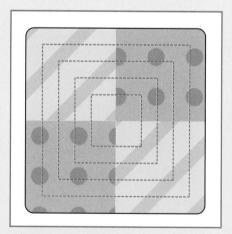

3 Place the backing and the patchwork squares RS together on the table. Put the batting square on top of both. Pin and stitch through all three layers on all four sides, leaving an opening of 1½ in [4 cm] on one side. Snip the corners to reduce bulk and turn RS out. Oversew the opening closed.

4 To quilt the coaster, machine stitch a line ¼ in [7 mm] in from the edge, marking this with pins or using the quilting foot as a guide.

5 For further quilting, mark parallel lines in from the previous ones and finish by stitching around the perimeter.

Repeat to make a total of 4 coasters.

PART THREE:
APPLIQUÉ METHODS AND TECHNIQUES

SCALING A DESIGN

Appliqué means "applied" and describes the technique of cutting a decorative shape from one fabric and stitching it to another, either by hand or machine *(see rear cover)*. This section describes various appliqué methods. Design ideas are to be found anywhere and everywhere, from wrapping paper or a child's coloring book to the internet.

However, the images we find are seldom the precise size that we want. Here is a basic method of scaling up and down for enlargement and reduction (reverse the size order in Steps 2 and 3 to make the image larger).

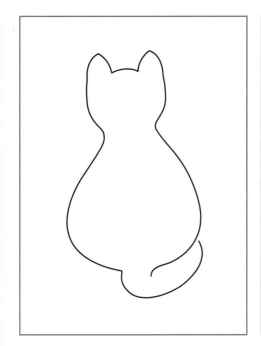

1 Trace or print out the original image.

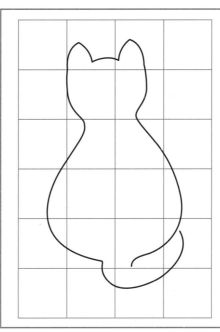

2 Enclose the outline image in a frame and divide the area into squares.

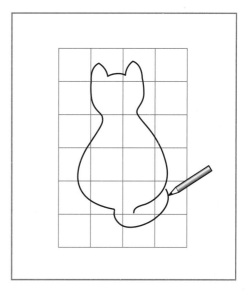

3 Rule up a smaller sheet into the same number of divisions and copy the original, square by square, until the reduced design is complete and ready to form a template.

Cutting out and sewing appliqué

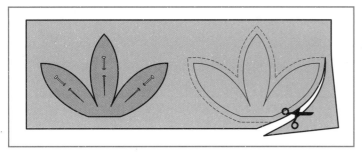

1 Pin the template to the fabric and trace round with a fabric marker. Cut out the shape with a ¼ in [7 mm] seam allowance; omit the allowance if planning to oversew (step 3).

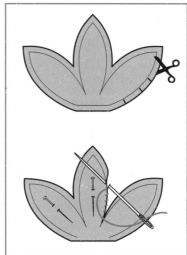

2 Clip the curves for a smooth edge when slip-stitching the appliqué to the base fabric. With a size 8 "sharps" needle and waxed quilting thread, turn the seam allowance under with the needle tip as you sew.

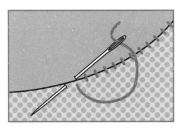

3 You can oversew the raw edges of the shape directly onto the base fabric. Stitch closely if it frays.

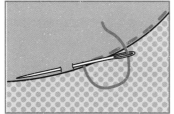

4 Running stitch can be used for attaching non-fraying material such as felt.

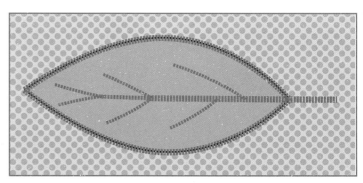

5 Appliqué by machine offers a choice of stitch effects, including zigzag and satin stitch.

Double-thickness appliqué

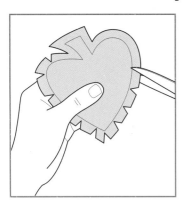

1 Pin two pieces of fabric RS together. Draw the motif on one side with a marker. Cut out with a ¼ in [7mm] seam allowance. Stitch along the drawn line, leaving a gap for turning. Clip the curves down to the stitch line.

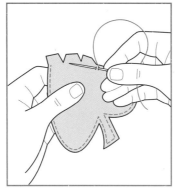

2 Turn RS out. Smooth the seam from inside with a crochet hook. Baste around the shape, closing the gap and folding in raw edges as you go. Stitch to the base fabric all round. Remove the basting.

1 Construct a single flower petal by pinning and sewing two pieces of fabric RS together. Leave open at the base. Clip the curves before turning RS out and press if necessary.

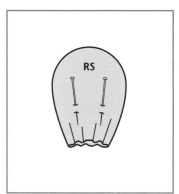

2 Pin the layers together and stitch gathers across the base. Make five petals and attach at the base only to the background, so they appear 3D. Sew a large fabric-covered button in the center.

USING FUSIBLE WEB

Fusible web is impregnated with heat-sensitive adhesive that sticks one piece of fabric to another when ironed.

It prevents the appliqué fraying and with the motif trimmed to shape, it keeps cut edges looking sharp without the need to turn them under. Some brands carry so much adhesive that it makes the fabric stiff and difficult to sew. Select one with a medium-strength bond.

Cut a piece of background fabric to the required size for your quilt block or project, including a ¼ in [7 mm] seam allowance. Select another fabric for the appliqué shape.

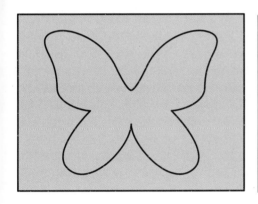

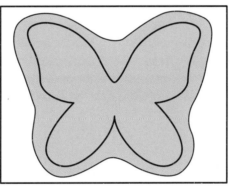

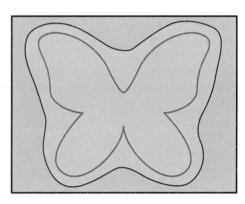

1 Draw or trace your motif onto the paper side of the fusible web. If it is an asymmetrical motif, make it a mirror image (reverse left to right).

2 With a margin of about ¼ in [7 mm], roughly cut the shape out of the fusible web.

3 Place the cut-out onto the WS of appliqué fabric, paper side uppermost, and iron to fuse the surfaces together. When cool, cut out carefully along the drawn lines.

Peel off the paper backing. There may be backing on both sides – brands vary, so do read the manufacturer's instructions. Position the prepared appliqué, RS up, on the background fabric and press again. Always use a pressing cloth to keep the adhesive off your iron.

Fusible web creates only a temporary bond, tending to lift and curl after washing. So it is still necessary to machine the appliquéd shape into place using satin stitch, blanket stitch or several lines of straight stitching.

USING FREEZER PAPER

Freezer paper, invented as food wrap but now available from quilting suppliers, will adhere to fabric when ironed shiny side down. It doesn't harm the iron and is the modern equivalent of using traditional paper templates cut from newspapers or old letters.

Freezer paper templates allow for greater accuracy and make the handling of shapes much easier. Quilters' freezer paper is also the right size for photocopiers and printers, so you can create multiples of any one shape. If using printer ink, check whether it is washable, in case it marks your fabric.

Preparing the shape

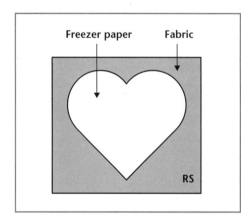

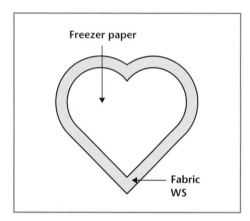

1 A heart shape is ideal for practice. Trace, draw, photocopy, or print onto the matt (non-shiny) side of the freezer paper then, on an ironing board, lay the paper shiny side down onto the RS of your fabric. Press with a hot dry iron. The paper will adhere to the fabric in a few seconds. Cut out the heart shape with a margin of ¼ in [7 mm] all round and peel off the paper.

2 Place the fabric heart WS up on the board and reposition the paper, shiny side up.

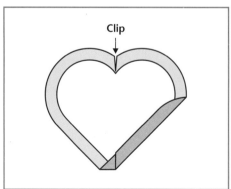

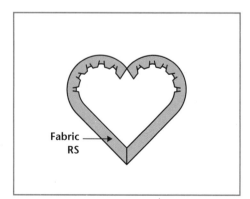

3 Press the point of the heart up with the tip or edge of the iron. Make sure it sticks to the paper.

4 Clip curves where necessary. Continue to press the foldover margin onto the paper all around the heart.

5 If the paper lifts away, reapply the iron and hold down the fold with your fingertips until the paper cools.

Attaching the shape

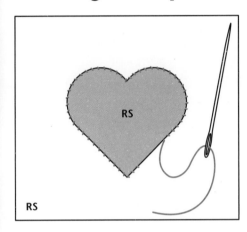

6 Pin the heart to the backing fabric, RS up. Sew with a stabbing motion, coming up through the appliquéd shape and going back down through the backing. The stitches should be quite close together. Avoid going through the freezer paper if possible, so that it can be more easily removed later. If you leave a gap of about 1 in [2.5 cm] you may be able to remove the paper from a small shape by working it out through the gap with a pair of tweezers. Finally, sew the gap shut.

Sewing by machine Use an appliqué foot (p. 35) if available, as it enables you to see where the stitches are. Set to a very small zigzag stitch, or use the machine hemstitch, which employs a sequence of several straight stitches, then a zigzag. With the hemstitch, the straight stitches should be in the background fabric only, as close as possible to the edge of the appliqué.

Removing the paper

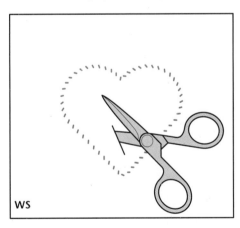

7 On the WS, cut a slit in the backing fabric and gently pull the freezer paper out through the slit. Be careful not to pierce the heart shape with the tip of the scissors. There is no real need to sew up this slit since the piece will either be lined or become the top layer of a quilt sandwich where the reverse will not be seen. Finally, press very lightly.

8 For larger areas, it is best to cut away all the backing fabric that lies immediately behind the appliqué, leaving a ¼ in [7 mm] seam allowance. Again, take care not to pierce the heart shape with the scissors. Gently pull out the freezer paper, not forgetting to strip out the pieces under the seam. Finally, press very lightly.

QUILTING APPLIQUÉD BLOCKS

Just like traditional patchwork, appliquéd blocks may be sewn together to form a quilt top.

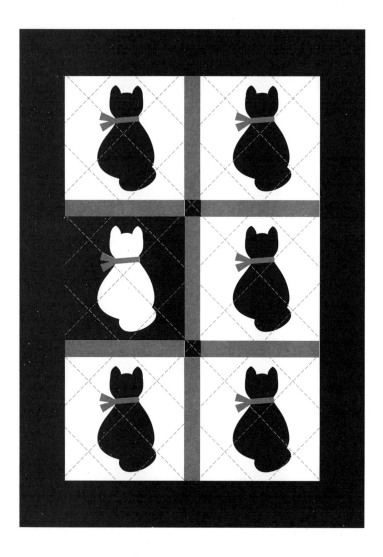

Instead of joining the blocks edge to edge, sashing (also called latticing) may be used, where narrow strips of fabric separate – and effectively frame – each motif (see illustration).

The whole quilt sandwich can then be assembled and quilted in straight lines, or by stitching around each motif, once or even several times (p. 20). If there are larger background areas not covered by appliqué, there's the possibility of using a filling pattern by the free motion machining method (p. 23).

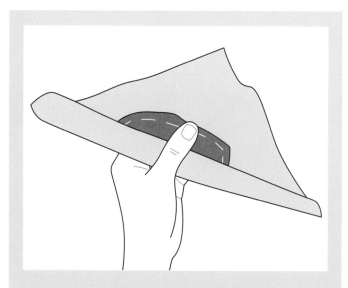

When sewing appliqué in hand, fold or roll the project in your free hand to get a good grip on the stitch area and keep your wrist straight to avoid a cramp in your thumb.

MACHINING APPLIQUÉ

Machine accessories

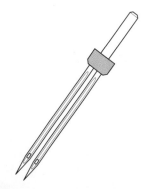

Open toe appliqué A useful variation on the standard zigzag foot, the widely-spaced toes on this foot afford a clear view of appliqué and quilting work.

Appliqué/embroidery The toes on this foot are shorter, for smoother stitching, improved visibility and maneuvrability.

Twin needle Requires two spools of top thread but interlocks with a single bobbin. The effect is two equidistant stitch lines on top and a zigzag beneath.

Threads

The range of synthetic machine threads includes metallics and "invisible" monofilaments. Take care not to melt synthetics when ironing. Some perform better than others, depending on the nylon or polyester filament; ask your supplier for recommendations. If using a cotton thread, choose a neutral color to blend with the backing fabric. However, one that contrasts with both backing and appliqué will accentuate the appliqué shape. Fine silk threads are excellent for hand sewing.

Tension

Regular machine stitching is formed by the top and lower threads interlocking in the fabric.

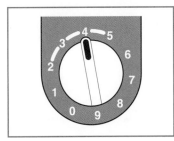

1 Top thread tension is governed by the tension dial, numbered 0–9. Behind it, the thread runs between two or three disks that are adjusted according to the dial.

2 Between 4 and 5 on the dial is considered "normal" tension. The threads meet in the center of the fabric and the stitching appears the same on each side.

3 Below 4, the tension disks loosen and the top thread runs more freely. The thread can then pass through both layers of fabric. This is only desirable if you want to create gathers by pulling up the bottom thread.

4 Above 5, the disks are screwed together more tightly and the reverse happens.

Most modern sewing machines produce a number of decorative embroidery stitches. Try one of these to stitch around a plain appliquéd shape.

When you have finished, leave long thread ends. Gently pull the bobbin thread on the WS, and a tiny loop of the top thread will appear. Pull this loop through to the WS and tie a knot with the bobbin thread. Now thread a needle with both threads and tidy them away with a couple of stitches into the back of the work.

PROJECT: FELT NEEDLECASE

This simple project is ideal for beginners. It makes a surprisingly durable and attractive item and a useful gift. It uses felt, which doesn't fray, so the motifs are easily cut out and appliquéd with a neat blanket stitch.

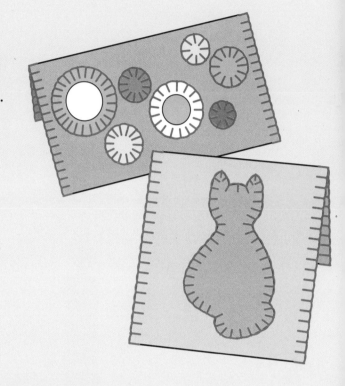

To make the felt needlecase you will need:

- Several sheets of wool-mixture felt, approx. 8 in [20 cm] square
- Flannel, felt or soft muslin for inner pages, approx. 8 in [20 cm] square
- Sewing thread for attaching pages to cover
- Stranded embroidery floss or pearl twist for edging and appliqué
- An embroidery needle
- Trimmings such as buttons or sequins
- Sharp scissors

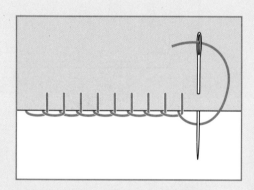

Blanket stitch Start with a knot, bring needle through to RS at stitch height and oversew fabric edge once, forming a loop. Pass needle through loop and pull tight against edge. Working from left to right, push needle into fabric again at same height. Pull needle forwards through new loop to form a half-hitch. Tighten as before. Repeat and fasten off with extra half-hitch around final loop.

Method

Cut a piece of felt, 4 x 8 in [10 x 20 cm]. Folded in half, this forms the cover of the finished case, 4 x 4 in [10 x 10 cm]. Buttonhole stitch all around the edge in a contrasting colored thread.

On paper, trace any of the motifs from the opposite page (or devise your own). Use them as templates to outline and cut out felt shapes, which will decorate the outer cover of the case.

Arrange and baste your chosen shapes onto the outer case, then blanket stitch them into position. Use a thread that contrasts with the appliqué motif.

For the inner "pages" – where the needles and pins go – cut one piece of felt, flannel or muslin, 3½ x 7¼ in [8.5 x 18.5 cm], and the second one smaller, 2⅝ x 6½ in [6.5 x 16.5 cm]. If you have pinking shears, prepare the pages with them to make a decorative zigzag edge and reduce fraying.

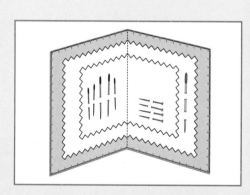

Open the cover out flat, WS up, and place the larger page on top of it with an equal margin all round. Next, place the smaller page on the larger one, again with an equal margin all round. Baste the three layers together down the center, from top to bottom, and then machine stitch them for permanence.

Cover the stitching if you wish, with a length of narrow ribbon that matches the color of the buttonhole edging. Tie it in a bow on the outer spine and secure with a couple of stitches through the center bow. Add any buttons, beads, sequins and so forth to the outer cover, if required.

MOTIFS FOR APPLIQUÉ

TRIMMINGS

Suitable trimmings include braid, ric-rac, cord, ribbon, bias binding and lace. Other embellishments include sequins, beads, buttons, shells and even dollshouse miniatures like tiny scissors.

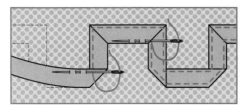

Outlining with braid Add emphasis to applied shapes by outlining them *(see rear cover)*. Braid may be sewn by hand or machine so long as it is done with precision and no wrinkles.

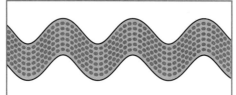

Ric-rac braid This narrow, flexible braid woven in zigzag formation is a popular basic trimming.

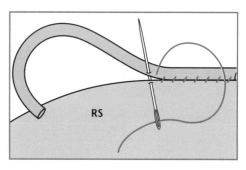

Outlining in cord Cord defines curves where straight braid cannot. It is slip-stitched by hand; the needle passes through the cord and picks up threads at the edge of the appliqué, pulling the two together.

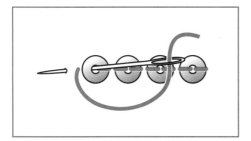

Applying sequins Secure the thread on the WS and bring the needle up through the eye of first sequin. Back stitch over the right-hand edge, come out on the left-hand edge and back stitch down through the eye. Advance a stitch and repeat with the next sequin.

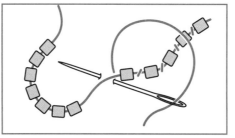

Applying beads Thread up two needles and secure both threads on the WS. Bring the first needle through and thread it with a number of beads. Take the second needle and stitch across the first thread coming through the first bead. Slide the second bead close to the first and repeat until all are in place.

Check that trimmings are safe to wash. If not, they would be better suited to wall-hangings than bed covers. Fabrics such as lace and ric-rac may be pre-shrunk by a warm-water soak beforehand. Take care when pressing any synthetics. Small embellishments – even buttons – that could be pulled off or swallowed should not go on a young child's quilt, although they could be used in a wall hanging that is kept out of reach.

Project ideas

- Create a mirror pair of quilted and appliquéd picture blocks – in the shape of a pet or cottage – and sew them together to form a novelty teacosy *(see rear cover)*.

- Make a draft stopper from a piece of fabric the width of a doorway and about 12 in [30 cm] deep. Sew several rows of braid, bias binding, ribbon and lace across it. Make casings at each end to take drawstrings. Sew up the long side to create a sausage shape. Thread and close one of the casings with a drawstring, stuff with batting, then repeat at the other end.

- Construct a personalized greetings card, using ribbon to appliqué a friend's name or flower motif onto a small piece of fabric. Attach this to the front of a blank card.

Wider ribbons or braid can make an effective border for a project, or use several rows of the same material such as ric-rac in graduated colors, for example a deep purple, dark blue and pastel blue.

PART FOUR:
ASSEMBLING A QUILT

A BASIC BORDER

The edging around a quilt top can be quite plain or worked as intricately as the top pattern itself. It can also be used to harmonize the colors it frames.

A basic border consists of four strips with no mitering at the corners. Cut to any width, it can be used to increase the overall quilt size without making extra patchwork or quilting work (see p. 42 and the classic frame quilt).

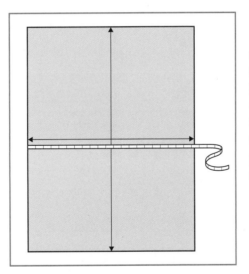

1 Measure across the middle in both directions. Cut four border strips, including a ¼ in [7mm] seam allowance. Cut two to the length of the patchwork; the other two to the same width plus that of two border strips (see step 3).

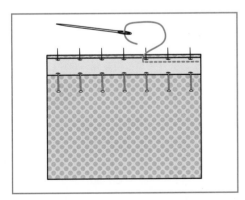

2 Take the lengthways strips first. Pin RS together to the midpoint, then outwards to either end. Baste firmly before stitching. Press.

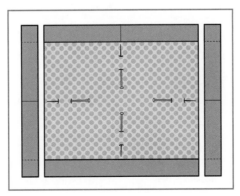

3 Line up the shorter strips, pin, and baste to the main piece as in Step 2.

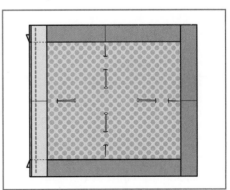

4 Sew the remaining strips straight across the ends of the first two, to form a square joint. Press.

FINISHING

Foldover edge

This is the simplest finish of all. Trim the top, batting and lining level all round. Fold the lining fabric and batting back together by ⅝ in [15 mm]. Pin or baste to hold them in position if necessary. Turn the top edge under once to meet the folded edge of the lining. Slip stitch the top and lining together.

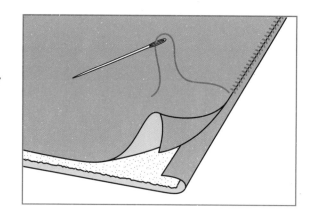

Self-bound edge

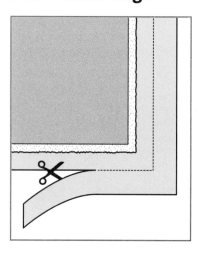

1 With the top and batting already trimmed level, cut the lining with an allowance of 1-2 in [2.5–5 cm] all round.

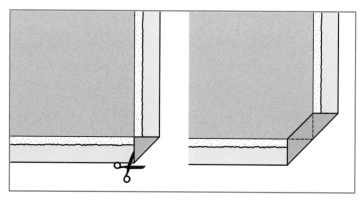

2 Fold, cut, and fold again each corner of the lining, in preparation for mitering.

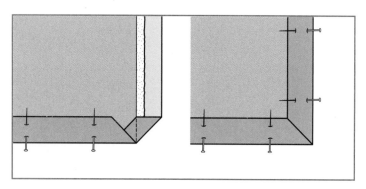

3 Fold the lining upward to meet the quilt top and form a self-binding. Turn the raw edges under and pin adjacent sides, with the corners meeting in a neat diagonal line.

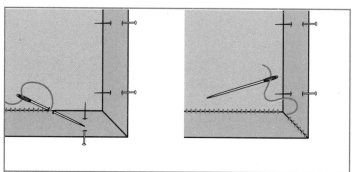

4 Using matching thread, slip-stitch the binding to the quilt top all round, closing each mitered corner as you go.

Straight-bound edge

Measure the quilt both ways and add 2 in [5 cm] to the length and width. On the grain (p. 8), cut four binding strips 1½–2 in [4–5 cm] wide. Press a turning of ¼ in [7 mm] down one side of each strip.

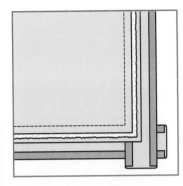 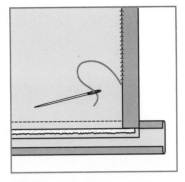 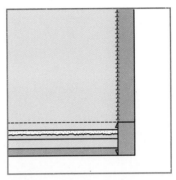 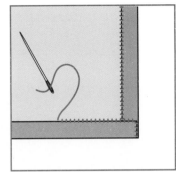

1 RS together, align the unturned edge with the raw edge of the quilt top. Machine stitch together with a ¼ in [7 mm] seam allowance. Prepare all four sides like this.

2 Fold the pressed edge of the binding over to the WS. Pin and slip-stitch the first length to the lining fabric, covering the initial stitch line.

3 Fold in the edge of the adjacent binding. Trim away bulk if necessary.

4 Fold the binding up to cover all raw edges. Slip-stitch to the lining fabric as in Step 2 and close the squared corner. Repeat around the quilt.

Bias-bound edge

Bias binding is often used on quilted items that cannot be neatened by turning. It can be homemade from steam-pressed bias strips to your chosen width, or bought readymade in various widths and materials.

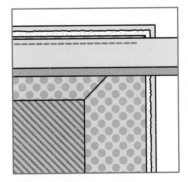 

1 Press open one side of the bias binding. RS together, align with the raw edge of the quilt top. Pin and stitch along the fold line of the binding.

2 Carry on sewing right round the quilt. The bias (p. 8) will stretch around the corners. Fold the binding over to the WS. Pin and slip-stitch to the lining fabric, covering the initial stitch line.

Signing your quilt

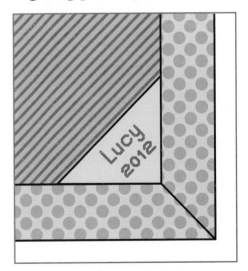

As a finishing touch, embroider your name and the date onto the quilt. Work it into the border, or make a separate label that can be slip-stitched to the lining or bound neatly into one corner, as shown here.

PROJECT: A CLASSIC FRAME QUILT

The "frame" quilt was a clever device of early quiltmakers for creating an eye-catching quilt when they had only a relatively small piece of an interesting printed fabric but a surplus of something more average-looking.

The quiltmaker would take the interesting piece of fabric as the center of the quilt top and use strips of complementary fabrics to "frame" it. Not only was this a pleasing way to feature a favorite fabric, it was also a very quick and simple way to make a quilt.

It is not necessary to use a novelty fabric as the center piece unless you have one you are keen to use. The project described here features quite an ordinary center panel but it is nevertheless an eye-catching quilt. You could substitute any fabrics to match a particular color scheme, if desired.

The finished quilt is approximately 40 in [100 cm] square. If you would like to make it larger, you need to add extra strips to the frame and enlarge the backing and batting accordingly. It can be sewn by hand or machine but would obviously take much less time using a sewing machine.

Use 100 percent cotton fabric and thread. The quantities below allow a little extra material for small cutting errors. All strips include a ¼ in [7 mm] seam allowance. The quilt top uses three different-patterned fabrics (A, B and C) and a fourth one (D) of equivalent texture and weight for the quilt backing. All fabrics involved should be preshrunk (p. 8).

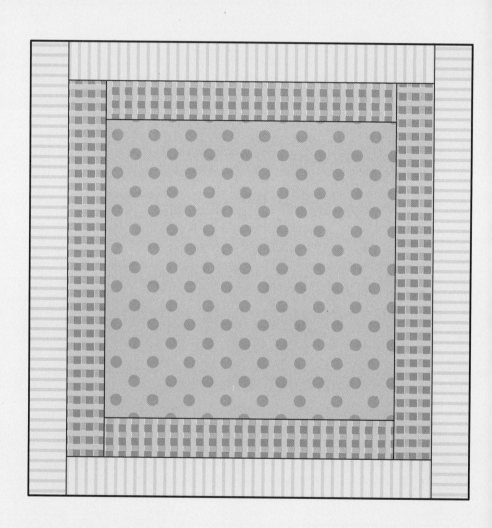

You will need:

- **Fabric A (spot)** One 26 in [66 cm] square, which forms the center panel
- **Fabric B (check/plaid)** 36 x 22 in [92 x 56 cm]
- **Fabric C (stripe)** 44 x 22 in [112 x 56 cm]
- **Fabric D (backing)** 44 in [112 cm] square
- **Batting** 44 in [112 cm] square (final size)
- Cotton thread for machine or hand sewing
- Embroidery thread and needle for tying

Method

Using your cutting mat, acrylic ruler and rotary cutter, from Fabric A cut out the central panel 24½ in [62.2 cm] square.

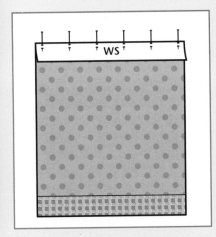

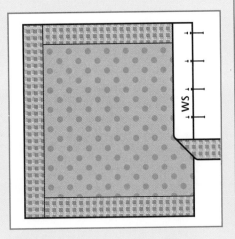

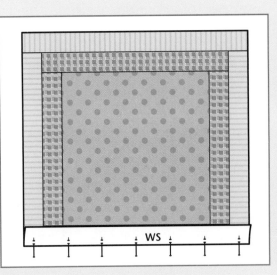

1 Cut two strips of Fabric B, 4½ x 24½ in [11.5 x 62.2 cm]. RS together, pin along two opposite sides of the central panel. Stitch both strips to the panel. Press seams outward toward the open edges.

2 Measure and cut two more strips of Fabric B, 4½ x 32½ in [11.5 x 82.5 cm]. As before, RS facing, pin then stitch the strips along the remaining two sides of the central panel. Press seams outward toward the open edges.

3 Take Fabric C, cut two strips 4½ x 32½ in [11.5 x 82.5 cm] and two more 4½ x 40½ in [11.5 x 103 cm]. Attach them in opposite pairs to the preceding frame, as for the central panel. Press seams outward and then press the entire quilt top.

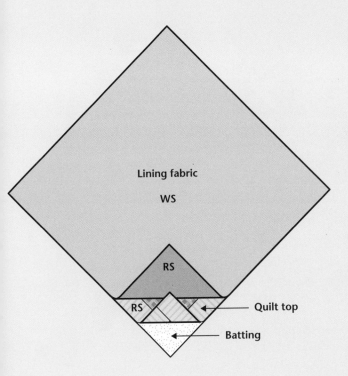

4 Measure and cut a piece 44 in [112 cm] square of the batting and also of the backing, Fabric D. Smooth out the batting and lay the quilt top RS up on top of it. The top will be slightly smaller all round than the batting. Place the piece of backing RS down onto the quilt top.

Pin the three layers all around the perimeter, smoothing them as you go, carefully aligning the edges of the quilt top with the backing. Stitch around the perimeter of the backing fabric with ¼ in [7 mm] seam allowance but leave an opening of about 12 in [30 cm]. Ensure you are sewing right through the quilt back, top and batting.

Use your rotary cutter, mat and ruler to trim any bits of batting protruding beyond the quilt top. Snip the four corners and turn it all RS out. Smooth all three layers outward from the center. Close the 12 in [30 cm] opening by hand.

Quilting

This quilt lends itself to tufting (p. 19) at intervals of 6 in [15 cm] along the seam lines and also on the front and central panel, which is the quickest method. Use the acrylic ruler to mark the quilt top at regular intervals. If you would like to quilt more ornately, choose template pattern(s) or filler lines (p. 22) and hand or machine quilt.

THE APPLIQUÉ TRADITION

Examples of appliqué exist from medieval times in Europe and the technique goes back as far as the Ancient Egyptians.

Although it can be utilitarian, a means to repair holes or tears, appliqué evolved into a decorative art as needleworkers became ever more imaginative, assisted by new products coming onto the market. The "album" quilt in North America was a special kind. Each block showed a picture on a particular subject, for example a Bible story, a political event or even a mourning quilt, to mark someone's death. More cheerfully, there were friendship album quilts, where friends contributed a block and embroidered their signatures. They often became a family's best quilts because so much time and thought went into making them.

Early appliqué shapes included ordinary domestic objects, simply traced around to provide a template: coins, scissors, eyeglasses or a spoon. Broderie Perse, popular in the eighteenth and nineteenth centuries in the UK and North America, consisted of cutting out figures featured on printed fabrics, to appliqué them onto and thus enhance a plain fabric. The name came from the belief that it resembled Persian embroidery.

The Rose of Sharon pattern frequently appeared on North American bridal quilts. Complex appliqué like this involves careful planning; the plans show the stitching order for the rose motif and swag border. Repeat shapes are cut from paper or card templates, based on original drafts on graph paper.

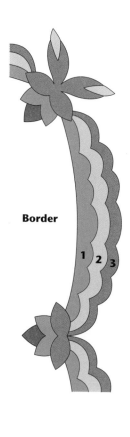

Border

Rose of Sharon motif

DISPLAY

To display your work as a wall hanging, maybe in an exhibition, you must have some way of suspending it. To construct a hanging "sleeve" or tube, you can either make it the width of the entire quilt or have several smaller ones. Using a fabric identical to or coordinating with the backing fabric, cut a strip 10 in [26 cm] deep and as wide as the quilt plus 4 in [10 cm] extra for hemming.

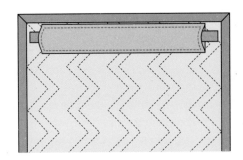

Create a tube by folding the fabric RS facing and sewing up the long side. Fold down the raw edges by 2 in [5 cm] at either end and hem stitch. Turn RS out and press so that the seam line will not be noticeable from the back of the quilt. Using a ruler, mark the line on the back of the quilt where you will attach the top of the sleeve, approximately 1–2 in [2.5–5 cm] from the top edge. You cannot machine the sleeve to the quilt, so you must attach it by hand with a suitable stitch such as regular running stitch, back stitch, slip-stitch or herringbone. First, sew the top of the sleeve across the width of the quilt then attach the lower side of the sleeve in the same way. Slide the supporting pole through the open ends. Vacuum clean your hangings regularly and take them down to shake outdoors from time to time.

Mounting

Small samplers of finely stitched quilting can be mounted and box framed to keep them clean. A roundel of Welsh or Amish design, quilted on plain fabric, shows up beautifully with the right light on it (*see rear cover photograph*).

Cut a mount from hardboard, card or foam board. Hardboard must be sawn but use a sharp craft knife for the others, together with a metal ruler and cutting mat.

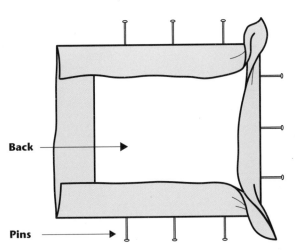

Back

Pins

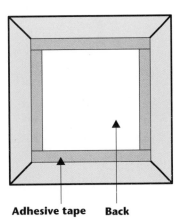

Adhesive tape **Back**

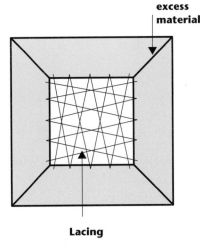

Folded excess material

Lacing

Lay the appliqué or quilting face down. If not padded already, put a layer of batting between the work and the mount. Always place the fabric against the rough side of the hardboard. The padding should not extend beyond the board but there should be a margin of fabric. Pull up and pin firmly to the board edges with long pins.

Hardboard will not take pins, so use adhesive tape. Fold the corners in and pull the fabric taut. Tape the fabric foldover to the back of the board. Do not stick adhesive tape onto or near stitched areas.

For lacing, fold the corners neatly and start lacing across the back from the middle of one of the shorter sides. Use strong thread and work a large herringbone stitch from side to side to avoid straining or distorting the fabric. Repeat across the two remaining sides.

AFTERCARE

Look for the care symbols on any fabric that you buy; the manufacturer's care label appears on the bolt and you should ask for a care ticket to take away with you. Other points of reference are your own washing machine and tumble dryer manuals.

An extensively hand-quilted project is better hand-washed, although it can be washed in a machine on a delicate cycle with a spin at low speed and dried outdoors. A quilt can be laundered in the bath, but to reduce the risk of the weight of water breaking threads when lifting out, put the quilt inside a single duvet cover. Squeeze out as much water as you can with your hands or feet, then let the duvet cover take the weight as you remove the quilt from the bath. Use clean towels to absorb some of the moisture and allow the quilt to dry outdoors on a sheet laid on the grass in warm weather, but place it in the shade as sun may cause certain colors to fade.

Synthetic batting is machine washable and can be tumble dried; make certain the quilt top and backing can be treated the same. On the other hand, cotton batting should always be pre-shrunk. Some quilters use it straight from the roll deliberately because when they wash the finished quilt, it will dry with an antique puckered effect.

If you have used lightweight woolens or silk in your quilting, and you want to wash it either by hand or machine, choose soap flakes or a liquid for delicates. The cleansing agents in liquid soaps are designed to work at low temperatures and won't leave a powdery deposit. Test strong colors (especially reds) for colorfastness and if in any doubt dry clean the quilt. Woolen or wool-mix fabrics of any kind should always be rinsed in warm water. Use the machine-washable wool setting on your machine, not the low-temperature or hand-wash program that delivers a cold rinse.

Tumble dryers are frequent contributors to accidental shrinkage; some fabrics are better left to dry without heat. Lift your quilt from the washing machine and use a clean towel to remove excess water. Lay the quilt to dry flat or drape it over a drying rack. If necessary, iron fabrics according to the recommended heat setting. Take extra care with trimmings; nylon lace, metallic threads, and plastic sequins will shrivel at the touch of a hot iron.

Dust, dirt, and perspiration harm fibers of all kinds and moths and molds feed readily on dirt. Put quilts away clean and dry, rolled or folded neatly in chests and cupboards, or inside zippered cotton covers for long-term storage. Shake them out occasionally and roll again or refold a different way to prevent permanent creases. Avoid the risk of mold or mildew by never storing fabrics in poorly ventilated, damp or humid surroundings such as lofts, basements or neglected cupboards. Low-powered heaters and dehumidifiers help to combat damp and condensation.

GLOSSARY

Appliqué The technique of stitching one fabric on top of another to create designs

Backing The quilt lining

Basting Temporary stitches made with running stitch, removed when work is finished

Batting Padding in the center layer of a quilt

Betweens Needles for fine stitching and quilting

Bias Any diagonal line between lengthwise and crosswise grains

Bias binding Packaged ready-made, in a variety of colors, it is useful for creating appliquéd shapes, especially curves, such as flower stems and basket handles

Block Pieced units sewn separately and later assembled into an overall pattern

Bodkin A blunt-tipped, large-eyed needle used for threading cord, ribbon and so on

Border Fabric edging or frame added to the top layer of a quilt

Broderie Perse The technique of cutting out a motif from a printed fabric in order to appliqué it onto a plain fabric. The term is French for "Persian embroidery"

Calico A plain white cotton cloth, sometimes unbleached, useful for quilt backings

Candlewick A soft, thick cotton embroidery thread

Contour quilting Where the parallel lines of quilt stitches are sewn approximately ¼ in [7mm] from the seam. Also called "outline stitching," it emphasizes the geometric shapes in a patchworked block

Cord A cord made from cotton, used in corded quilting. Can be bought by the yard

Echo quilting Where the quilting lines echo the outline of each appliquéd shape or patchwork piece. Similar to contour quilting

Fat quarter Half a yard of fabric cut off the bolt then cut in half again along the lengthwise grain to produce a rectangle

Feed-dogs Tiny metal teeth that move the fabric from front to back as machine stitching proceeds

Felt Non-woven fabric made from compressed fibers. Better quality felt contains wool. Available in many bright colors but bright sunlight will cause some fading in time

Free motion quilting A method of machine quilting with the feed-dogs lowered. It produces filling stitches rapidly

Filling Padding sewn between quilt top and backing

Filling stitch A quilting stitch used to cover larger areas of fabric. Can be done by hand or machine

Freezer paper Originally a food wrap, used by quilters to create appliquéd shapes

Fusible web Iron-on synthetic bonding material, useful for appliqué

Grain Direction in which the warp and weft threads lie

Hawaiian motif A formalized style of appliqué where intricate designs, cut from folded paper, are used as a template to make an appliquéd motif sewn onto a white background and frequently echo-stitched

Hem Folded and stitched edge, to prevent fraying

In the ditch Quilting stitches made in the center of the seam

Interfacing Extra fabric sewn or ironed between fabric layers to provide more body

Isometric paper Paper printed in a grid of equilateral triangles, useful for devising patchwork patterns

Jump stitch A stitch taken to "jump" across a join or from one part of a design to another, particularly when "in the ditch" or contour quilting

Kantha A type of embroidery originating in India, consisting primarily of a running stitch. The name comes from "kontha," meaning "rags" in ancient Sanskrit

Lawn A fine cotton fabric with a soft feel

Latticing Narrow strips used to separate quilt blocks. Also called "sashing"

Miter Corner pieces joined at an angle of 45 degrees

Motif A distinctive design element

Glossary continued:

Muslin A sheer, loose-woven cotton fabric. In the US, it is the name given to calico and various sturdy cotton fabrics of plain weave that are good for quilt backings

Nap Texture or design that runs in one direction only

Needle (verb) To stitch or stab with a needle

Notch Small triangular cutouts in the seam allowance, for aligning pieces when sewing

Patch A shaped piece of fabric, often cut out with the aid of a template for patchwork

Patchwork Fabric shapes or patches sewn together in a set design

Pearl thread Shiny cotton embroidery twist, non-divisible

Piecing Joining fabric shapes or patches together

Pile Soft raised surface on velvet, corduroy etc. (see **Nap**)

Post Small square piece at the junction of sashing/lattice strips

Press Often used for "ironing" but more strictly involves steam and a pressing cloth

Presser foot Part of the needle assembly that holds fabric flat while the machine needle makes stitches

Quilt Bed cover consisting of two layers of fabric with padding sewn or tied between

Quilting Action of stitching the three layers of a quilt together

Quilting hoop Portable frame for holding a portion of quilt while stitching

RS Right side of fabric

Reverse appliqué A technique where several layers of fabric are put together then parts of the upper layer(s) are cut away to reveal those below (see rear cover).

Ric rac A type of zig-zag braiding, useful for appliqué

Rose of Sharon A complex appliqué pattern of floral motifs and swags, popular in US bridal quilts

Rotary cutter A very sharp tool with replaceable blades of various diameters, used for cutting fabric strips and trimming wadding

Sashiko Traditional Japanese type of embroidery

Sashing Narrow strips used to separate quilt blocks. Also called "latticing"

Scaling Proportional enlargement or reduction of a design

Seam allowance Distance between the cut edge and the seam line

Seam ripper Small sharp tool for removing machine stitching

Selvage Solid edge of a woven fabric

Seminole Strip-pieced technique often used for borders

Setting in Fitting one piece into an angle formed by two others already joined

Sharps General sewing needles

Slip stitch Attaches a folded edge to a flat surface

String Technique of creating a solid fabric from sewn strips

Strip Technique of pattern-building based on strips of fabric rather than blocks

Template An outline guide for tracing and cutting

Tension Refers to the pressure placed on the needle and bobbin thread by the sewing machine and registered by two types of tension: the thread and bobbin tensions. Read your sewing machine manual for specifics

Top Patterned top layer of a patchwork quilt

Trapunto A stuffed quilting technique where motifs are padded so they appear in relief against the background fabric

Tufted Method of securing quilt layers with knots of thread

Vilene See **Interfacing**

WS Wrong side of fabric

Warp Runs lengthwise, parallel to the selvage

Weft Runs at right-angles to the selvage